AF261228
VAN GOGH
IRISES
12 SHEETS SINGLE-SIDED
SCRAPBOOKING DESIGNS FOR CRAFTS
SCRAPBOOK PAPER PAD
6x6, NON-PERFORATED SHEETS
© Crafty As Ever

TO REMOVE CUT ALONG THE DOTTED LINE.

TO REMOVE CUT ALONG THE DOTTED LINE.

www.ingramcontent.com/pod-product-compliance
Lightning Source LLC
Chambersburg PA
CBHW042141030726

47599CB00002B/574